A New True Book

APATOSAURUS

By Dave Petersen

CHILDRENS PRESS®

CHICAGO

Dinosaur bones at Dinosaur National Monument

Allen County Public Library
Ft. Wayne, Indiana

PHOTO CREDITS
Art—Richard Wahl—4 (bottom), 45
American Museum of Natural History—
  #2417 (Cover), p. 6
  #PK212 p. 4 (top)
  #120381 p. 10
  #2421 p. 15, p. 20 (left)
  #2580 p. 17
  #PK159 p. 18 (left)
  #125160 p. 22 (right)
  #324393 p. 22 (left)
  #2884 p. 26
  #844 p. 35 (right)
MARTIN BRUCE/ Shostal Associates, Inc.—20 (right)
Carnegie Museum of Natural History—29, 33 (top & bottom), 39
Dinosaur National Monument/Shostal Associates, Inc.—2
Used With Permission From Dinosaur Nature Association—35 (left), 37 (right), 42, 45
Field Museum of Natural History—9, 13, 31
STEWART M. GREEN/Tom Stack & Associates—34, 40
MILAN HERZOG/Shostal Associates, Inc.—16
RAY MANLEY/Shostal Associates, Inc.—18 (right)
AP/Wide World Photos, Inc.—25, 37 (left)

Library of Congress Cataloging-in-Publication Data

Petersen, David.
  Apatosaurus / by David Petersen.
    p.   cm.—(A New true book)
  Includes index.
  Summary: Describes the characteristics of the dinosaur with the long neck and tail, how its name was changed from Brontosaurus to Apatosaurus, and the discovery of dinosaur bones by paleontologists.
  ISBN 0-516-01159-6
  1. Apatosaurus—Juvenile literature.
[1. Apatosaurus.] I. Title.
QE862.S3P46   1989   88-37654
567.9'7—dc19   CIP
                                      AC

TABLE OF CONTENTS

Tyrannosaurus rex (above) had a large head filled
with sharp teeth. It was a meat eater. The Apatosaurus (below)
was much bigger than Tyrannosaurus rex, but it was
a plant eater. Look at the modern horse
and you can see how huge
both dinosaurs were.

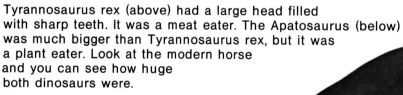

TYRANNOSAURUS
REX

MODERN HORSE

APATOSAURUS

APATOSAURUS

What do you think of
when you hear the word
"dinosaur?" Many people
think of Tyrannosaurus rex,
"king of the tyrant lizards."
However, another
dinosaur—Apatosaurus—is
more well known. It was
not a tyrant. It was a gentle
giant that ate plants.
Apatosaurus was much
bigger than Tyrannosaurus
rex. It grew up to 76 feet

Apatosaurus once was called Brontosaurus.

long. That's as long as a
train car. It weighed 30
tons (60 thousand pounds).
That's as heavy as 20
large automobiles.

Like many other dinosaurs,
Apatosaurus lived about 140

to 150 million years ago,
during a time known as
the Jurassic Period.

If you drew a picture of
this dinosaur, you probably
wouldn't call it Apatosaurus.
That's because for years
Apatosaurus was called
Brontosaurus.

Brontosaurus means
"thunder lizard." Someone
thought this dinosaur was
so huge that it must have
made the ground boom
like thunder as it walked.

THE DECEPTIVE LIZARD

How did one dinosaur get two names? And why did dinosaur scientists— called paleontologists— finally decide that Apatosaurus is the better name of the two?

When scientists want to name a newly discovered plant or animal (living or extinct), they have to follow certain rules.

One of these rules says that the first, or earliest, name given to the plant or animal becomes its official scientific name.

Sometimes, though, the same animal is discovered and named by more than one person.

Bryan Patterson was with the Field Museum's expedition to western Colorado in 1939.

In 1937 Charles H. Coles drew this Apatosaurus.

That's what happened with Apatosaurus. After it was discovered and named, another scientist found more bones in a different place and chose his own name. That name was Brontosaurus.

For years, scientists thought that Brontosaurus and Apatosaurus were closely related but different dinosaurs. Somehow, the name Brontosaurus became well known. The name Apatosaurus, which means "deceptive lizard," was rarely used by anyone except paleontologists.

When it was finally decided that Brontosaurus and Apatosaurus were the same creature, something had to be done about its two names. Apatosaurus was the first name it had been given. Therefore, it became the official name.

This mural by Charles R. Knight shows an Apatosaurus
moving toward waters surrounded by prehistoric crocodilians.

GETTING TO KNOW
APATOSAURUS

The Apatosaurus was a
large, plant-eating dinosaur.
Once, it was thought
that Apatosaurus lived in the
water most of the time.

It seemed that the Apatosaurus's body was so huge that its legs would not have been able to support its weight on land. Living in water would take much of the weight off its legs.

Also, it was once thought that its twenty-foot neck might have been used as a snorkel. If this were true, Apatosaurus would have been able to walk in deep

Apatosaurus was a member of a group of dinosaurs that scientists call sauropods. All sauropods were plant eaters.

water, eating plants that grew on the bottom. From time to time, it could lift its head up above the surface to breathe.

Now scientists know that this could not have been.

The skeleton and feet of
Apatosaurus were not like
those of animals that live
most of the time in water.
Water-dwelling animals,
such as the hippopotamus,
have shallow rib cages
and short, weak legs. Their
toes splay, or spread, to

Hippo mother with her calf

Apatosaurus
foot bones

support their weight on
soft mud.

Apatosaurus, on the
other hand, had long,
strong legs. Its rib cage
was deep, and its feet
were padded for walking
on dry ground. Because of

17

Apatosaurus skeleton (left). Apatosaurus was like an elephant (right) in some ways. It was not afraid of water, but it did not live in water.

these facts, scientists now believe that Apatosaurus was more like an elephant than a hippo.

Like an elephant, Apatosaurus probably roamed the countryside in herds, eating pine needles and leaves.

The size and shape of
the dinosaur's teeth
support this theory. Their
extreme wear is further
evidence that Apatosaurus
ate leaves and other land
plants.

Finally, fossil remains of
water plants are not found
where sauropod bones are
found. The remains of tall
trees, however, often are
common.

Thus, Apatosaurus used
its long neck as a giraffe

Apatosaurus (left) and giraffe (right)

uses its neck—to reach up into trees for leaves.

Apatosaurus and the other sauropods, therefore, can be thought of as the elephants and giraffes of the dinosaur world.

ON THE TRAIL
OF APATOSAURUS

Scientists learned about
Apatosaurus and other
sauropods through
"ichnology." This is the
study of fossilized footprints.

In many places, dinosaur
tracks were left in mud.
Later, this mud hardened
and turned to stone.

When Richard T. Bird photographed these footprints (left), he said they looked as if they were left by a herd of "cows going down a country lane." As you can see from the molds (right), these footprints were huge.

One trail was found by a scientist named R. T. Bird, in Bandera County, Texas. This trail showed the tracks of 23 sauropods, all traveling together.

Oddly, no tail-drag marks are found in any of the sauropod trails. This leads scientists to believe that Apatosaurus carried its twenty-foot tail up off the ground.

Apatosaurus probably spent most of its time eating. It would have taken a lot of leaves to feed such a huge body every day.

This means they probably ate fast and didn't chew their food very well.

Therefore, they may have used "gastroliths." These are stones that some dinosaurs swallowed to help grind up food in their stomachs.

Scientists have found gastroliths among the remains of sauropods.

Another old belief about dinosaurs that's changing

Scientists pieced together this dinosaur egg. See how much bigger it is than the chicken's egg at the right.

is that all dinosaurs were egg-laying reptiles.

Since fossilized dinosaur eggs have been found, we know that some of them *did* lay eggs.

However, scientists now

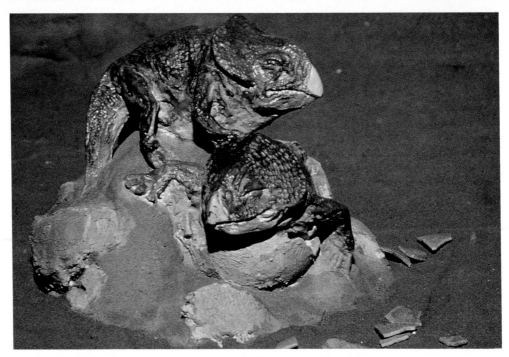

Scientists know that Protoceratops babies hatched from eggs.

feel that some dinosaurs were born alive. Were Apatosaurus' babies hatched from eggs or born alive? No one knows.

Scientists are still looking for the answer to this question.

BRAIN SIZE

For all its great size, the brain of Apatosaurus was about as big as a baseball. This means it probably wasn't very bright.

Scientists once felt that such a tiny brain would also limit Apatosaurus to slow body movements.

However, most researchers today think this is wrong. The structure of the Apatosaurus skeleton indicates that it would have moved like an elephant—slowly much of the time, but able to run and make other quick movements.

The Carnegie Museum of Natural History in Pennsylvania
displays the Apatosaurus skeleton found by Earl Douglass.

DISCOVERY

The man who first found and named Apatosaurus was Dr. Othniel Charles Marsh. He was one of the most famous "dinosaur hunters" of all time.

In the early 1870s, a man who worked for Dr. Marsh found some huge dinosaur bones in Colorado. These bones were new to Dr. Marsh. They were the biggest bones he had ever seen.

Dr. Marsh worked for
the Peabody Museum
of Natural History
at Yale University
in New Haven,
Connecticut. He sent
workers to Colorado
to look for
dinosaur bones.

So, in 1877, Marsh sent
a large work crew to
Colorado to dig up more
of the big bones.

Dr. Marsh named this new dinosaur, Apatosaurus.

In 1909, another dinosaur hunter—Earl Douglass— also made an important find.

In a hill of sandstone at Split Mountain in Utah Douglass found a line of eight giant tail bones. The tail bones turned out to be connected to a nearly complete skeleton of Apatosaurus. Only the head and a few other parts were missing.

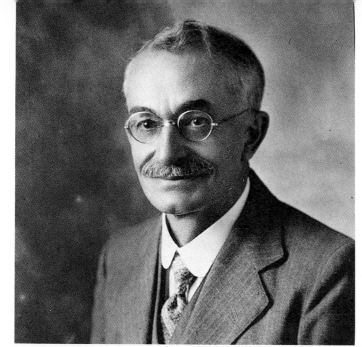

Earl Douglass (left) worked for the Carnegie Museum of Natural History in Pennsylvania. He discovered dinosaur bones along the Green River in Utah at a place called Split Mountain.

Split Mountain was home to many dinosaurs.

Douglass shipped the bones to the Carnegie Museum in Pennsylvania. There, they were cleaned, repaired, sorted, and fitted together.

Apatosaurus wasn't the only dinosaur Douglass and his workers found at Split Mountain. Others were Allosaurus, Camptosaurus, Diplodocus, Laosaurus, and Stegosaurus.

Model of a life-size Stegosaurus (left) and Camptosaurus skeleton (below)

CHANGING HEADS

In addition to having two names, Apatosaurus until 1979 also had two heads.

That's because, to this day, no skull has been found directly attached to an Apatosaurus skeleton.

For twenty years the Apatosaurus skeleton that Douglass found was shown without a head. Then,

Camarasaurus skull and its recontruction (right)
For many years, this skull shape was used on Apatosaurus.

based on the theory of
Dr. Marsh, a Camarasaurus
skull was placed on the
Apatosaurus skeleton. Some
scientists said this skull
was the correct one. But
many scientists disagreed.

37

It was not until 1979 that paleontologists settled the question. On October 20, Apatosaurus got its new head. The head was based on the skull Douglass had uncovered seventy years earlier.

This skull is small, long, thin, and somewhat horselike. Its teeth are peglike.

Since the skull was not directly attached to the

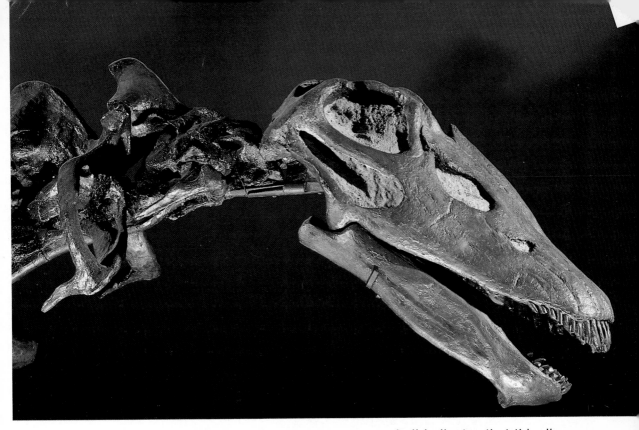

The shape of the Apatosaurus skull indicates that this dinosaur probably had good senses of sight, smell, and hearing.

Apatosaurus skeleton, scientists can't be positive that it belongs. Still, the evidence suggests that the skull and skeleton belong together.

Split Mountain Gorge in Utah

DINOSAUR
NATIONAL MONUMENT

In 1915, Douglass's discovery was protected for the people.

On October 4, 1915, President Woodrow Wilson declared the land surrounding Split Mountain a national monument.

Visitors Center at Dinosaur National Monument

Today, thousands of visitors a year go to this dinosaur graveyard and see paleontologists at work.

How did so many dinosaurs come to be buried in this one hill? Did they all die

here at the same time,
killed by some great
disaster? A flood, or
maybe an earthquake?

Douglass didn't think
so. He believed that
140 million years ago,
Split Mountain was a flat
sandbar located at a bend
in a river. Over a great
many years, the bodies of
dinosaurs that died upriver
were washed down and
left on this sandbar.

As the bodies became
skeletons, they were buried

by more sand. Gradually,
the bones under the
sand became fossilized.

Much later, geological
forces pushed the
hardened sandbar upward.
Erosion from wind and rain
formed the hill now called
Split Mountain. All of this,
of course, took millions
of years to happen.

For those of us who
love dinosaurs, there's no
place quite as interesting as
Dinosaur National Monument.

Maybe someday you will
visit this exciting place
yourself.

Apatosaurus will be
waiting there for you.

WORDS YOU SHOULD KNOW

crocodilian(krahk • ah • DIL • ee • yan) — one of a group of reptiles like the alligator and crocodile, having long jaws, a long tail, and short legs

deceptive(dih • SEP • tihv) — misleading; not what it seems to be

dinosaur(DINE • ah • sore) — any of a group of extinct animals that dominated the earth many millions of years ago; some grew to enormous size

erosion(e • ROH • jun) — the wearing away of the earth by the action of wind and water

extinct(ex • TINKT) — no longer living

fossilized(FAWSS • il • ized) — turned into a fossil, the hardened remains of a plant or animal that lived long ago

gastrolith(GAS • tra • lith) — a stone swallowed by an animal to help it grind and digest its food

geological forces (gee • ah • LAHJ • ih • kil FOR • sez) — movements of the earth that cause changes in the height and shape of the land

ichnology(ik • NAHL • uh • gee) — the study of hardened remains of the footprints of animals that lived long ago

Jurassic Period(joo • RASS • ik PEER • ee • ud) — the name for a period in the earth's history that lasted from 180 million years ago to 130 million years ago

paleontologist(pail • ee • en • TAHL • uh • jist) — a scientist who studies the fossil remains of life from past periods of the earth's history

reptile(REP • tyle) — an air-breathing, cold-blooded animal (such as a snake or lizard) that is covered with scales or bony plates and that has very short legs or no legs at all

sauropod(SORE • uh • pod) — a group of plant-eating dinosaurs that had a long neck and tail and a small head

snorkel(SNORE • kil) — a tube that reaches the surface, used by divers to breathe underwater

tyrant(TIE • rent) — a harsh ruler who has complete power and who is often cruel and unjust

INDEX

About the Author

David Petersen is a senior editor for Mother Earth News *magazine, and author of* Among the Elk *(Northland Publishing Company, 1988). He has written eight titles in the True Book series.*